POEMS
AND SONGS

Jocelyn Hyppolite
jvhyppolite@yahoo.com

Cover : "Harmony" by Serge Dor (painter, sculptor and musician), reproduced with the artist permission.

Editions Saint-Hubert
fsainthubert@yahoo.com

Jocelyn Hyppolite
jvhyppolite@yahoo.com

Editions Saint-Hubert
fsainthubert@yahoo.com

Cover: "Harmony" by
Serge Dor (painter, sculptor and musician) reproduced with the artist permission.

Print information available on the last page.

ISBN: 978-1-4251-1732-0 (sc)

Trafford rev. 08/06/2021

 www.trafford.com

North America & international
toll-free: 844-688-6899 (USA & Canada)
fax: 812 355 4082

Table of contents

In memory of my beloved parents who passed away too soon:

**Michelson Paul Hyppolite
and
Marie-Claire Jourdan Hyppolite**

Marie-Claire Jourdan
Hyppolite
(1921 - 1998)

Me Michelson
Paul
Hyppolite
(1910 - 1991)

Préface

Jacques Viélot

Victor Joseph Rafael Jocelyn Hyppolite was born March 23, 1945 in Port au Prince, Haiti. Jocelyn, as he is known, came to us as a proud member of the Bas Peu de Chose clan. We were teenagers when we met and I don't regret it.

Jocelyn and I are friends and comrades and share many important political and personal experiences together. I feel undeservedly honored to have been asked to write the preface for Jocelyn's book of poetry and songs. At the same time I find myself in a somewhat uneasy situation as I am not, nor do I pretend to be, a literary critic. What I do know is that it is extremely difficult to translate a poem from the original language to another language without the original loosing much of its poetic integrity. The challenge confronting me revealed, I will proceed with an effort to do justice for the work of my esteemed comrade.

Certainly poetry involves both "inspiration" and "genius." I believe the same may be said for song writing. In his book Jocelyn has mastered written verse in both lyrical and narrative forms. His verses, just like the masters that he read and studied as a child - Jean de Lafontaine, for example - carry a clear and distinct ethical message and as well, they tell a story. At times one must delve deeply into the crevices of Jocelyn's compositions to fully understand the precise and recognizable message within his creation. For those of us who enjoy a mental challenge, Jocelyn, we can thank you for the provision.

At the same time, Jocelyn has stated that he has no objection to the reader or listener abstracting his or her own message from his works, giving one the freedom of his own interpretation and canon of criticism. This, it seems to me, allows us to have our cake and eat it too. How sweet it is. It could not get better.

Poets and song writers are formed and they pick out from the events of daily life the subjects of their creations. Jocelyn would let it be known that his style in both genres is greatly influenced by his French counterpart, Jacques Prévert. Then too, Jocelyn's father, a man of letter, must have had a profound influence on Jocelyn. No doubt Jocelyn heard spoken of or read some of his father's works and was stricken by what he perceived as his father's brilliance. The admiration he felt for his father's intellectual accomplishments seems to have served as an impetus for Jocelyn to match, which he successfully does.

It is incontrovertible that the late Gérard Michel was Jocelyn's music mentor and friend. The association of the two, Jocelyn and Gérard, circumscribes his experience and knowledge of music. Consequently, it is possible that Michelson Paul, Jocelyn's father, might not have played a significant role in Jocelyn's music but only served to spur him on.

Jocelyn writes about and sings his emotions as a child would. He is frank to a fault, as is demonstrated in the lines of his poem, Loneliness, where he opens a window on a facet of his life that he normally tries to hide. We find the same thing in the poem, My Son, whereas the poem, Je vous salue en la patrie, touches on a different kind and level of personal relationships. The latter being a tribute to his dear friends and comrades who were cowardly and senselessly murdered for political and ideological reasons under the Duvalier dictatorship.

In dealing with political themes, Jocelyn's poetry encompasses both the tragic and the comic, legitimately so. It is up to the reader to be the judge. What is an absolute about Jocelyn's work is his ability to deal equally well with the creative as well as to critically analyze the chosen subject. Hence, we can easily conclude that Jocelyn is, indeed, simultaneously both the poet and the song writer.

Jacques Viélot

Poems and Songs

INTRODUCTION

I hope that my profound love for the American people, and consequently, the rest of humanity is not lost on those of you who peruse through the pages of this booklet.

Of course, my love for humanity, beauty and harmony clashes with the injustice that is so prevalent in our world. Also, my hatred of injustice extends to those who perpetrate it.

I like to talk about peace. However, I believe like the philosopher W.F. Hegel that peace is a 'blank page" in history. Nonetheless, peace can become a goal for humanity as a whole if it is preceded by a necessary social "war". The purpose of the war in question is to dismantle the dehumanizing social system in which we live and that strives my hatred along with its oppressive legal system.

I cannot over emphasize my love and affection for the American people and want them to know that my disgust and hatred for their government's foreign policy is no reflection on them. The US government alienates the rest of the world but the American people do not.

Of course, not many understand the implications for humanity of the global capitalist system; a system that evolved and was framed by greedy beast like masterminds. This is why it requires tremendous efforts by many to unravel the seeming mystery of its mechanisms and comprehend the inner logic that lie underneath the complexity and extent of its relations.

My wish is as follows. The time shall come when the American people will come together harmoniously, rise up against and overthrow the oppressive machinery of capitalism, and restore the best that humanity can offer to the benefits of all. Only then would we have eradicated the basis nay-the servants-, of this evil.

Furthermore , the Bush's will take to the bushes like rabbits as the best of humanity will coalesce and ride the tidal waves of evolutionary changes like blooming wild flowers.

I wish to thank all those who had helped me with the manuscript of this book. First and foremost, I want to thank without comments and qualifications my lovely wife and children, Joselyne, Marvin, Noundy and Naima. My long time friends and comrades Jacques Vielot who wrote the thought provoking preface, and Francis Saint Hubert who edited this book, as he did the previous one. Of course, this volume contains some translated material from the French book. Those are included because I believe they should be made available to the English speaking reader. Francis Saint-Hubert is the accomplished and talented musician who prepared the sheets music for this book. I also want to thank two of my coworkers, Juan Navarro and Maxo Rimpel who graciously provided the illustrations. Particular thanks go to Charmaine Borda and Michelle Karshan for proof- reading the text. To all those who encouraged me along, especially Jocelyn Gay, Romain Morisset and Mona Lou Teeter, I say *merci*.

JOCELYN

BELLE

You are
now mature!
Belle means pretty
do you know?
I think you do
Belle is your essence
You can imitate ugliness
You will never come close!
Because Belle
is your nature
Yes "jolie" you are
lovely, loving and love-able
Wisdom comes with
Experience, brings maturity
Should you be happy?
Yes indeed!
And I am too for you!

THE PROMISE

Be sure to call me!
Yes I will!
Are you sure?
Yes I am
I called, we talked
I called, we talked
I called, we talked
five times, six times
I wrote you a poem
a lovely one
discribing your natural
and inner beauty
I called, we talked
You said that
you will let me know
your thoughts later
you will call me?
Yes I will
You will call me?
Yes I will
You will call me?
Yes I will
While awaiting for the call
a destroying anguish
raised my heartbeat
now full of anxiety

I kind of know then
That you will never call
Because you never did before!
Nevertheless I waited
and waited,and waited
and waited,
and waited still!...
You did not call !

I kind of know now
That you will never call back
Nevertheless I waited
And waited, and waited
And waited, and waited still !
You did not call.
It's unfortunate that
You never did!...

MARIA

Working in the bag-room
Under the hot FLORIDA's sun
With some blowing fans
To dry the salty sweat
Of hard labor clerks
Even though for the wind
You have no love,
No passion, MARIA
Don't cut off the power switch
To our fans.
Let the wind blow for us.
Let the wind blow por favor.
Let the wind blow some more.
Pretty please MARIA
My pretty, pretty friend
Let the wind blow today,
Tomorrow
forever and a day maybe.

THE BEAUTY

Beautiful, beautiful
Feeling of fairy tales
Pretty angel walking the earth
Dressing in white
With no visible wings
Powerful, polite and gentle
Troubled, I look at her
With grace, she looks at me
A smile enlightens her face
Revealing mine, frozen
With total admiration!
And the silence erupted!
She turned and kept on walking
With that smile
That never ends
In my astonished eyes.

Loneliness

I should be loving you tonight
Social duties commanded me
To get involve in certain fights
I can't be there when you want me

When once a week we had a chance
Get together to share a day
As we execute our love dance
Our son walks in and wants to play

We never have a cool day for Marvin
Togetherness is only in our mind
When you get home I'm out to the wind
When I come back the time we cannot find

You fell asleep mostly by loneliness
Waiting for my love, my mistreated friend
To carry you to that mountain
We want so bad of happiness

You thought I did not understand
Perhaps not noticing a thing
It hurt me bad my awereness
I felt inside my loneliness

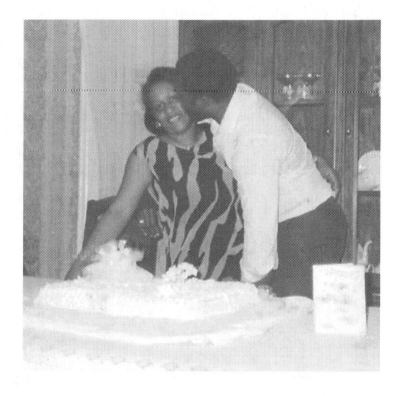

Loneliness

Lyrics and music by:
Jocelyn Hyppolite

Loneliness

I can't be there when you want
our son walks in and wants to

me.
play.

We ne-ver have a

cool day for Mar-vin

to-get-her-ness is

on-ly in our mind.

When you get home I'm

out to the wind

when I come back the

Written and harmonized by:
Francis Saint-Hubert

DIALOGUE

Are you from here?
No, I am not.
Where are you from?
Haiti!
Oh! How fortunate you are!
Why, if I may ask?
Oh! It 's a beautiful country!
It has a warm climate!
So?
What do you mean: so?
Is that enough
To make a country beautiful?
Well I must admit
The masses are poor!
And?
And you have a dictatorship!
Well supported by
The U.S. government!
What's new?
Our government is always
On the wrong side
Of the fence!
I don't know what to say?
You have said it right
Thank you,
For being clairevoyant.

Awareness

I ought to sing
My pain and yours
I ought to sing our misery
So that you can be free
Of a world of lies,
Corruption, tricks
And deceptions
I ought to sing our "*happiness*"
Free of lies, anger
And sorrow
Full of morality and ethics
Even though
We are chained between
Life and death
Because life and death
Are the two masters
That enslave us
Too attached to life
Too tired to fight

My son

You want to play
And run in the park
It's wintertime
The trees are bare
Of all their brown leaves

I know you're sad
It's like being incarcerated
To stay home constantly
The snow is falling
All I can do is to protect you

Let's go to sleep
Dream of the future
Don't feel so bad
And let us hope
To see tomorrow

Let me hug you my son
And warm you with my heart
The spring is waking up
And summer will be soon

Now you have grown

The feeling is deeper
I'm very proud
You are my son, the Gentleman
I've always dreamed of

Life hasn't changed much
I'm waging a battle
Still to that future best
We escaped the snow
The cold New York too

Sleep a little
Dream a little
Don't be fooled
By the future
Past and present
Are realities
Future is a concept

Let me hug you my son
And warm you with my heart
Winter is in the past
And summer is present

My son

Lyrics and music by:
Jocelyn Hyppolite

My son

car - ce - rat - ed   to   stay home cons - tant -
ly.   The snow is   fall -ing,   all I can
do   is to pro-tect   you.   Let's go to
sleep, dream of the fu - ture.   Don't feel so

Chorus

bad,   and let us   hope   to see to-mor -

row.   Let me hug you my

son,   and warm you with my

heart,   the spring is wak-ing   up

and sum-mer will be   soon.   Now — have

Fine   DS 3x. Last time al Fine

Written and harmonized by
Francis Saint-Hubert

Noundy

Noundy at last you are now born
Noundy we have waited all so long
Noundy if you knew what we felt
Those tears and fears that we went through

Noundy we love you, love you much
Let us teach you the dance of life, are you ready
To make those very crazy steps, Noundy my love

One, two, three, four (ter) to the right
One, two, three, four (ter) to the left

Noundy we'll try to do our best
Noundy don't expect very much
We're poor in a foreign country
It is not free like they said

Noundy no matter what life will cost
Noundy we have to live somehow
Let's dance some more while life is still on
Noundy my dear

One, two, three, four (ter) to the right
One, two, three, four (ter) to the left

Noundy forgive us would you please
We had no right to have you born
in our miserable simple life.
Oh, sweet Noundy

Noundy we love you, love you much
Let us teach you the dance of life, are you ready
To make those crazy steps, Noundy my love

One, two, three, four (ter) to the right
One, two, three, four (ter) to the left

Noundy

Lyrics and music by:
Jocelyn Hyppolite

Noun - dy   at

last you are now born _____ Noun-

dy   we've wait-ed all so   long, _____

—   Noun - dy   if

you knew what we felt those

tears and fears that we went

through. _____ Noun - dy we

love you love you much _____ Let

us teach you the dance of life.

Are you rea-

dy to make those ve - ry cra-zy

steps, Noun-dy my love

One two three four, one two three four,

one two three four, to the right.

Noundy

One two three four, one two three four,

one two three four, to the left. —

to the left. _____

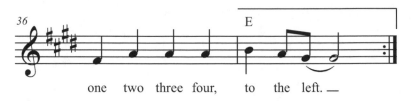

Written and harmonized by:
Francis Saint-Hubert

Decency

Hospital
Hospitality
Caring doctors
Working nurses
For sick patients
Industries blooming
Drugs causing sickness
Sickness making drugs
Wow! What a business

Caring family
Concerned family
Liquidating their assets
Savings of hard labor
Paying for drugs
Paying for loved ones
Buying pain off
Buying time off
Of assured death

Hospital
Hospitality
Working doctors
Caring nurses
Dying patients

17

Caring family
Concerned family
Liquidating life savings
To bill collectors
Life insurance
Insurance of life or death
Beneficiaries relieved
Sick business
Funeral homes
Gravediggers
Cemetery business
-Wow! What an industry!

Hospital
Hospitality
My dad is lying ill
His life is sliding
Slowly to his death
He could not speak
Not even write
His last word to me
Indeed he is gone
Without a word
I felt so bad
Worthless diminished
Days after weeks
Weeks after months
Months after year

Until today
I received
Your balance bill!

Hospital
Hospitality
You want to stir up
From my blood
Sixty more freaking pain
Cynical bill collectors
Cynical Grave Diggers
Caring doctors
Working nurses
Or vice versa

All I know
My dad is dead!
Damn it!
My dad is dead!
And you owe me
For failing to bring him
Back to me
Alive and Well

The Officials

Distinguished people
Well dressed and mannered
Talking suave
Talking sweet
Talking neat
Talking sharp

Promises, promises
Wearing the mask
Of innocence
False appearance
Is a must!!!

Disgusted liars
Cheaters, deceitful
Corrupted officials
Disguised by friendly smile
Voluble orators
Amazing "conscious-less"
Shameless, audacious
No limited arrogance
Slave Masters, dictators

Is that your democracy?

The officials

World of lies

North Atlantic Treaty
Organization
Of American States
European Union
Society of Nations
League of Nations
United Nations
Peace keeping forces
MINUSTAH forces
To better the world!?
Different names
For some kind of
Killing machines
Killing humans
Killing hope
Without life
Without hope

Go ahead, take the war
To the Middle East
They don't need
Nuclear weapons
In fact we objected!
We love them defenseless

Great opportunity
For thieves like us
With our war
Airplanes, our bombs
And missiles
Ironically weapons
Of mass destruction
We will shed their blood
Take their oil
We don't need
To pay for this
In money term that is!
We can trade
American life for it
It's cheaper!
Blood for oil
Oil for blood

I am the president
The commander in chief
I can do that
Gamble life, trading life
American life, youngster's life
Eighteen to twenty
In their prime, as bait!!!
I can do that!
I am the president!
The commander in chief
Food for oil
Oil for food

From Iraqi oil
To American life
From American Blood
To Iraqi life
Falling oil
Falling blood
To the soil of democracy
Lied your world
Of lies to all nations on earth
Commander in chief
You are the man!
The UN never validated
Your action
That should make you a felon
An assassin, a murderer
A terrorist commander in chief
You are the man!

The international war criminal
Along with Mister Blair!
You are now growing madder
And maddest
You have bugged America!
Every single affair
Became public knowledge now
Commander in chief
Tell me when?
When?
Your judgment is due?

25

Go away

Go Away
Go away
Do you hear me?
Go away
With your God
Or your Devil-God
Go away
With your forgiveness
Your sin
Or your forgiveness sin
Go away
Go away
With your heaven
Your dream
Or your dream heaven
Go away
With your Paradise
Your hell
Or your hell-Paradise
Go away
With your nonsense
Your sickness
Or your stupidity
And in the name
Of bread, life and love
Amen

CONVERSATION

RELAX
God is in control!

That is precisely
What's worrying me!

What do you mean?

Well, it's scary when
Nobody is in control!

REMEMBER...
Any time you talk
About God, spirit or
Things of the sort
You are dealing with
ABSTRACTION!!!

I am a simple man

I have no need for luxury
No need for eccentricity
Only basic necessities
I am a simple man

I need to breathe like everyone
I need to feel like everyone
To be happy like everyone
I am a simple man

I am human I have my pride
I am human won't you agree
I am human I know how to fight
I know how to cry and how to love

I need to work like everyone
A place to live like everyone
Commodities like everyone
I am a simple man

I need to eat like everyone
Need to feel free like everyone
Self-sufficient like everyone
I am a simple man

I am human I have my pride
I am human won't you agree
I am human I know how to fight
I know how to cry and how to love

I need to be proud of myself
And lay out my principles
I have morals, I have ethics
I am a simple man

If you try to deny me that
If you deprive me of my rights
If you're abusing me of my goodness
I'll show you my madness

I am a simple man.

I am a simple man

Words and music by:
Jocelyn Hyppolite

I have no need for lux - u - ry,
I need to breathe like e - very one

no need for ec - cen - tri - ci - ty,
I need to feel like e - very one,

on - ly ba - sic ne - ces - si - ties
to be hap - py like e - very one,

I am a sim - ple man

I am a simple man

Written and harmonized by
Francis Saint-Hubert

A song out of them

What is happening to our lives?
What is happening to our dreams?
Everything is computerized
And friendship has no meaning

Let us not talk of sanity
Or even worse, civility
We no longer have standards
Even our law is unbalanced
My dear friends

In the streets we are like singing birds
The summer swings within our blood
We are like that garden of love
Showered by fall flowers
We cannot escape from those torments
And the pain is breaking our heart
We took them all in harmony
And made a song out of them

We look for work here, everywhere
Experiencing fear on a dark alley
Trying hard to create a way
Looking for the expecting goal

One has seen Progress Century
One has seen Century of Lights
And been discriminated against
We could not hold those sad tears
My dear friends

To live our lives within the pain
We build a spirit of joy
A paradise blooming of lights
Yes, a playland free from darkness

To bring happiness to others
We have created beautiful thoughts
We have made more wonderful songs
And we have sung to everyone
My dear friends

Gérard Michel and friends : Lionel Oriol and Jean Prophète (keyboard).

A song out of them

Words and music:
Jocelyn Hyppolite

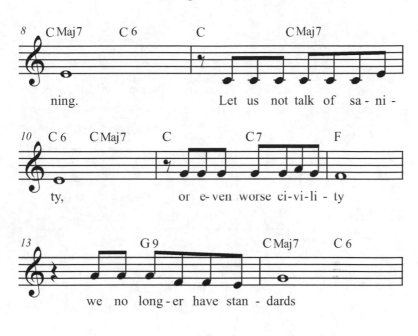

8 C Maj7　　C 6　　　　C　　　　C Maj7

ning.　　　　　Let us not talk of sa - ni -

10 C 6　C Maj7　　C　　　　C 7　　　　F

ty,　　　　or e - ven worse ci-vi-li - ty

13　　　　G 9　　　　C Maj7　　C 6

we no long - er have stan - dards

15 D m　　　D m7　　　　G　　D m7

e - ven our law is un - ba - lanced,　my　dear

17 G 7　　　　　Chorus
　　　　　　　　C　　　　C 7

friends.　　　In　the street we　are　like　sing -
　　　　　　　We　can - not　es - cape from those

3

A song out of them

19 F   D m   G 7

ing   birds,   the   sum -mer   swings   wi - thin   our
tor - ments   and   the   pain   is   break - ing   our

21 C Maj7   C 6   A 7/C♯

blood.   We   are   like   that   gar - den   of
heart   We   took   them   all   in   har - mo -

23 D m   D m7/C   G/B   G 7   C Maj7   C 6

love
ny   show-ered   by   those   fall   flow - ers.

CODA
(after last verse)

26 G⁷/B   G 7   C *To Verse*

and   made   a   song   out-of   them.

Written and harmonized by:
Francis Saint-Hubert

Decision

Tormented life

Of sensible souvenirs

Past or Present

Dead or Alive

It's our choice

Condemned

Honesty, morality
amazing thoughts
Taught by thieves
Corrupted officials
To mold ourselves
in their ways
And their needs
Tragic reality
We learned honesty
Condemned by morality
Frozen by shame
Overloaded
With responsibilities
They taught us acceptance

We learned tolerance
Tolerate exploitation
Carried domination
On our tired shoulders
Survival of the fittest

They said
Self-preservation one said
Oh well, we know
One is entitled
To his presumed
Right to exist
Dying for life
Living dead
Dying lives
On and on
Because happiness
Is a luxury thought
My friend

Fly my illusions

I remember those thoughts
When I was a teenager
Wonderful thoughts of freedom
I learned from the grownups
I found out sometime later
Adults have lied to us
They live in a world of make believe
And have made life unbearable

Fly, fly my illusions. Fly, fly my beliefs
Fly, fly my dreams. Fly, fly my hope.

I learned to love my country
To work for its well being
Struggled for its freedom
And being imposed occupation
We built jails and gas chambers
We provide death to our brothers' land
We hate, we kill, we love, we cry
We are so weak, we are so weak

Fly my illusions

Lyrics and music:
Jocelyn Hyppolite

I re- mem-ber those thoughts,

I was a teen - a - ger

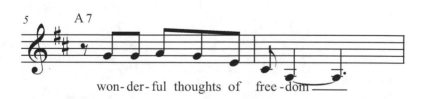

won-der-ful thoughts of free -dom

I learned from the grown - ups.

Fly fly my illusions

I found out some-time la - ter _____

a - dults have lied to us, they live in a

world of make be - lieve and have made

life un-bear-a - ble. Fly, fly

Chorus

my il - lusions fly, fly my be-liefs

fly,   fly   my dreams ——   fly,   fly my

hope.

Written and harmonized by:
Francis Saint-Hubert

Workers

Good people
Fighters, strugglers
Moral, loyal, decent
Ethical, hard to die
Working hard
Feeling pain
Working hard
sweating pain
Too honest to steal
Too exhausted to try
Too scared to get caught
Working hard
Feeling pain
Working hard
Sweating pain
Working hard
to the end
End of time
End of life
For loving
For caring
Builders, planners
Backbone of the society
Exploited and trashed
My love goes out to you

Only by Revolution

You want to overcome
This situation of unjust misery
There are no ifs, no buts in this matter
FIGHT FOR REVOLUTION!

Revolution is the only solution
To reach Democracy
Don't you let a liar tell you otherwise!
FIGHT FOR REVOLUTION!

Let us unite, yes we must stand
Let's organize for all events
Let's walk together to the sun
Revolution has just begun

We have been fooled before
By ruling masters throughout history
We have been mutilated through slavery time
Since we cannot forget

The weeping, the raping and the killing
Fighting scary nightmares
I am still hearing my ancestors
Crying out for their lives

We survived slavery time
And civil right, banned illiteracy
We still have a racist America
Apartheid South Africa

We must keep on the fight
We have no choice in order to survive
Anyone who tell you anything different
Is avoiding reality yeah!

Only by revolution

**Lyrics and music by
Jocelyn Hyppolite**

You want to o - ver-
There are no ifs, no

come this si - tua - tion
buts in this___ mat - ter:

of un - just mi - se - ry
fight for re - vo - lu - tion.

Re-vo-lu-tion is the on - ly___ so-lu-tion

Only by revolution

to reach de- mo- cra - cy

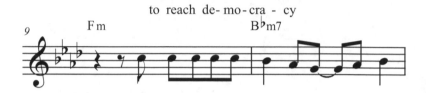

don't you let a liar tell you o - ther-wise

fight for re - vo - lu - tion.

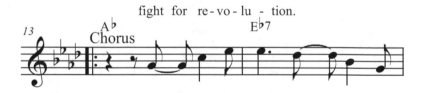

Let — us u - nite, yes — we must

stand. Let's — or - ga - nize for — all e -

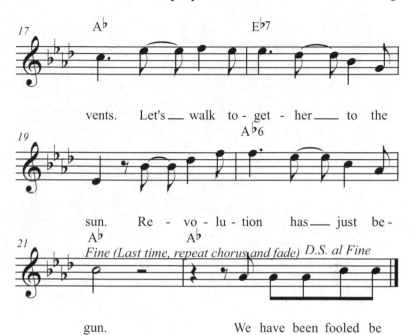

vents. Let's __ walk to - get - her __ to the

sun. Re - vo - lu - tion has __ just be -

gun. We have been fooled be

Written and harmonized by
Francis Saint-Hubert

Apology

Apology
Mister president
That's nice
Nice gestures
Mister president
Is apologizing
Yes sir
I am impressed

Beat me, whip me
Kick me
Feed me to the dogs
And apologize to me

What a great gesture
The big man
Is apologizing
This is the best event
Of the century
That's fine

Rape me, sell me
Use me as free labor
Eat my food, drink my coffee
And apologize to me

Apology my F
Apology my A
Mister president

You know
It's hard for one
To be respectful
When one's intelligence
Has been insulted

The slave trade
Is part of your libraries
And every nation history
Part of your school system
Part of your work force
Mister president

Upon recognition
Of a crime shouldn't
Reparation be in order?
It is basic decency
Mister president.

If in your mind
The word: *reparation*
Does not click
Hear this instead

Apologize <u>me</u>
Before you apologize <u>to</u> me
Do you know?
What I'm saying?
Mister president

The damage is enormous
My dignity
My essence of being
Has been walked upon
From past centuries
Until now
Do you know
What I'm saying?

Otherwise
Apology my F
Apology my A
Mister president

Scandal

In my deep sleep
I heard noises, voices
Voices from beyond
Abruptly I woke up
Like coming back
From a dream
And "whoop, whoop"
Barked the dogs
"Stop the robber"
Screamed the do-it-all maid

A woman
Under a mango tree
Was picking up
A few fruits fallen the night before
And "whoop, whoop"
Barked the dogs
"Stop this robber"
Screamed the do-it-all maid

The woman
Climbed back over the wall
She counted her treasures
In her folded dress
One, two, three, four,

Five, six little mangoes
And "whoop, whoop"
Barked the dogs
"Stop this robber"
Screamed the do-it-all maid

The woman
Slowly crossed the street corner
Under the bright light posts
Like nothing ever happened
And 'whoop, whoop"
Barked the dogs
"Stop this robber"
Screamed the do-it-all maid

A name

Freighter Arawak
Sun II
Speed to Freedom
Year 1991
To the land of Liberty
The land of the free
The land of opportunity
With Alfred Ismé,
Caught
and welcomed
with the chains
Of humiliation
His first taste of
American democracy

When I'll be me

I left my country in search of freedom
I miss my home so beautiful
My friends so nice, my sea so blue
And my sun so shiny

I came to New York much disillusioned
So many thoughts haunted my mind
Freedom is used on our emotions
But no such thing is free

But one day I will sing
I was that one they told, "Get the dolly"
One day I will sing
I was the one they told to sweep the floor
One day they will know

What kind of man I am
What kind of man I am, when I'll be me

I drove forklift, I carried bags and boxes
And through my heart I said, "I will make it"
I have read signs, which said, "Like it or leave it"
I closed my eyes so as not to see

I have been treated anyhow; I was a number
I felt so flat, small and worthless
Without respect, without any dignity
Gosh! I cried on my pillow

When I'll be me

**Lyrics and music:
Jocelyn Hyppolite**

When I'll be me

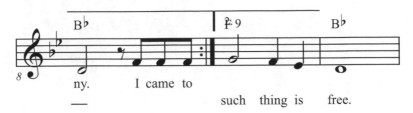

ny.   I came to   such   thing is   free.

But   one   day   I   will   sing

I   was   that one they   told   get   the   dol-ly

One   day   I   will   sing

I   was   the   one   they   told   to   sweep   the floor.

One   day   they   will   know

what   kind   of   man   I   am,

what kind of man   I   am,   when I'll   be

me.   I   drove fork

Written and harmonized by:
Francis Saint-Hubert

Je vous salue en la Patrie

For the hungry dear friend
Living in poverty
Who compromised his soul
For a better living

Je vous salue en la Patrie (bis)

For the comrade and friend
Who chose not to suffer
And crossed over the line
To serve the enemy

Je vous salue en la Patrie (bis)

For the lost little kids
And those mothers in tears
For those fathers who died

Je vous salue en la Patrie (bis)

For my friend Jean Vilson
For Emar Jean Francois
And for Eden Germain
Killed for saying no

Je vous salue en la Patrie (bis)

49

For the Barraud brothers
Little Doudou Creve Coeur
Yves Lindor choked to death
In the trunk of a car

Je vous salue en la Patrie (bis)

For the beaten comrade
By the Cayo Lobos Police
For comrade who took the boat
And never reached Miami

Je vous salue en la Patrie (bis)

For those outdoor macoutes
And those undercover
Rotten politicians
Who have destroyed my country

Je vous salue en la Patrie (bis)

Je vous salue en la Patrie

Lyrics and music by:
Jocelyn Hyppolite

For the   hun-gry dearfriend   li - ving
For the   comrade and friend   who chose

in po-ver-ty   who com - promised his soul   for   a
not to suf-fer   and crossed   o - ver the line   to serve

bet-ter li-ving, je vous sa - lue en la pa-trie, je vous sa-
the e-ne-my je vous sa   lue en la pa-trie je vous sa-

lue en la pa-trie
lue en la pa-trie —————   For the lost lit-tle

Je vous salue en la Patrie

kids ———————— and those mo- thers in

tears ———————— for those fa - thers who

died ———————— je vous sa-

lue en la pa - trie. ———————— For the

Written and harmonized by
Francis Saint-Hubert

Little Woman

Lovely night living in my memory
Sweet wonderful dream hope without an end
You will wake up in a sun shiny day
Sweet my little wish. You're my future best.

Oh, you my little woman, you my tenderness sweet.
You're the cause of my pain, also my happiness
You're my little woman; you're my fairy blue bird
You have vibrated my music and captured my soul

My poor heart is calling for that happiness
My dear being is burning of a too deep love
Coming O dear sunshine bring me joyfulness
Chase that dirty gloom in my troubled heart

Little woman

Lyrics and music:
Jocelyn Hyppolite

Love-ly night liv-ing in my

me-mo-ry —— sweet won-der-ful dream, hope wi-thout an

end. You will wake up in a sun

shin-ing day ——sweet my lit-tle wish you're my fu-ture

Little Woman

Little Woman

in my trou- bled heart. ——

Written and harmonized by:
Francis Saint-Hubert

Sad Morning

Oh! My love

If you knew how I feel
You would not leave me alone
I'm afraid for our love

Oh! My love

This death that comes over me
This ghost that haunts my dreams
Is breaking my heart

You and I

Sat on a mound of grass
Glancing at a hot sunshine
Which lighted our faces

If I go

If my days on earth pass by
I would go with my misery
You would be set free

Sad morning

Lyrics and music by:
Jocelyn Hyppolite

Oh my love if —— you know how I feel, you ——wouldnot —— leave me a- lone —— I'm —— a - fraid for —— our love.

Written and harmonized by
Francis Saint-Hubert

Adore You

Won't you believe I can love you truly
Won't you believe my eyes can adore you
Won't you believe my love for you is deep
My heart is breaking and I lost faith my dear
In this confusing dream

You have been mislead and I forgive you dear
I am getting lost, yes lost in this nightmare
Listen to me but not to the rumors
Because those rumors will close your heart to me
You are too dear to me

Adore you, yes adore you
Adore you my dear sweet love

If you would like to just give me a chance
I would bring you on top of the mountains
And we will live our true love to the end
Inside the Eden that Garden Paradise
In perfect Harmony

Adore you, yes adore you
Adore you my dear sweet love

Adore you

Words and music by:
Jocelyn Hyppolite

Adore you

you?
mare.

Won't you be-lieve my love for you is
Lis-ten to me but not to the ru-

deep?
mors,

My heart is
be-cause those

break-ing,____
ru-mors____

and I lost
will close your

faith my dear in this con-fus-ing dream.
heart to me, you are too dear to me. -

Chorus

A-dore you, yes a-dore

you   a- dore you   my dear sweet
-        -   -   -   -   -   -
love   a - dore   love.
-        -   -   -   -   -   -   -   -
-       -   -   -   -   if   you   would

Written and harmonized by:
Francis Saint-Hubert

Nobody Knows

Nobody knows how much I love her
Nobody knows how much pain is in my heart
How much suffering I had to go through
Nobody knows how much I love her

In all my thoughts and plans
She has the most important part
Because she is and will always be mine,
My dear beloved

Nobody knows that I have moonless nights
Nobody knows my heart has some sunless days
Nobody knows that I am dying slowly
Nobody knows how much I love her

In all my thoughts and plan
She has the most important part
Because she is and will always
Be mine, my dear beloved

Nobody knows how many nights I have been blue
Nobody knows how many days my heart went sorrow
Nobody knows that I am dying slowly
Nobody knows how much I love her

Nobody knows

**Words and lyrics by
Jocelyn Hyppolite**

Nobody knows

ing   I had to go   through   no- bo- dy

knows   how   much   I love   her.   In all my

thoughts   and plans she   has   the most im-

por - tant part   be - cause   she is and

will   al-ways   be   mine   my dear be-

Written and harmonized by:
Francis Saint-Hubert

Sunshine

My dear people
Please hear me out today
I came to you with
Very simple facts
Tell you this time
United we must stand
And we will see through the night
Shining a better day

Let me tell you
How much you're worth to me
You are my dream
We 're from the same country
Haiti is us
We must not forget that
We can make her much better
For all of us to be

This is the truth,
The very simple truth
I love you all

I love my country
When I hear of you my dear Haiti,
I can vision
Your sun so pretty

Sunshine I'm expecting
Sunshine for my country
Sunshine I'm demanding
Sunshine yes indeed

Let me show you
My sympathy for you
My deep concern
For your troubled soul
My sweetest hope
For your dream to hold on
And your children to be able
To share it too

Sunshine

**Lyrics and music by:
Jocelyn Hyppolite**

My dear peo- ple —— please hear me
Let me tell you —— how much you're

out to - day, ——
worth to me ——

I came to you —— with ve - ry
you are my dream —— we're from the

sim - ple facts. ——
same coun - try ——

Sunshine

'Tell   you   this   time ___   u - ni - ted
Hai - ti   is   us ___   we   must   not

we   must   stand   and   we   will
for   get   that   we   can   make

see through the   night ___ shin-ing   a   bet - ter
her   much bet - ter ___   for   all   of   us   to

day.
be.   This   is   the   truth, ___ ve - ry   sim -

ple   truth. ___   I   love   you   all ___   I   love   my

coun - try _____

When I hear of ___ you my dear Hai-ti ____

I can vi - sion ___ your sun so pret-ty. ___

Sun shine _____ sun-shine I'm ex -

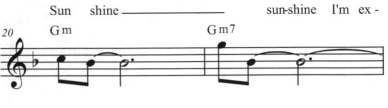

pect - ing. ___ Sun shine, _____

Sunshine

sun shine for my   coun try. ——

Sun shine, —————— sun shine I'm de-

mand - ing, —— sun - shine ——————

— sun-shine yes   in - deed.

Written and harmonized by
Francis Saint-Hubert

Victoria

She's a tough woman
Born on a small island
She does everything
A man usually does

She plays midfielder
On a women's soccer team
And she'll play rough
When it becomes necessary

She stands tall and proud
She is a woman
A strong woman
Who came from my country

She has four children
From a broken marriage
She fights very hard
To feed them everyday

She is a nurse's aid
She directs traffic and drives a van
She works three jobs
Trying hard to make ends meet

Victoria,
Her name says it all
She's a brave woman
She is a victory

She's got personality,
Vision, and maturity
And when she smilcs
Happiness floats all over

Victoria

**Words and music:
Jocelyn Hyppolite**

Victoria

does.   She plays mid- field -   -   -

er   on a   wo-man soc-cer   team

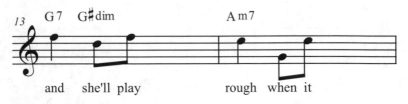

and   she'll play   rough when it

be-comes   ne - ces-sa -   -   - ry.

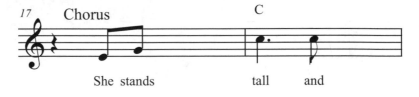

She stands   tall   and

Written and harmonized by:
Francis Saint-Hubert

Haiti is our own

Some of you like our songs
And some of you do not
It's your right however,
We only sing for you

Whether you're pleased or not
Whether you are hurt or not
Our major priority
Is to sing reality

Let us be, let us breathe
That's the name of our song
That's how strong we want life
That's how hard we will fight
Let us be, let us breathe
That's the name of our song

We don't need intruders
Haiti is our own
We have nothing to sell
Wholesale or in retail

We want our simple life
We want our little fun
We're fed up with
Your way of civilization

Haiti has a problem
For us only to solve
We can find our way out
We have had enough of your help

Thank you bloody Uncle Sam
For your imperialism
Get out of our land
Haiti is our own

We have been together
In our past way of life
All we now have to do
Redefine our planning

Revolution is a must
To clean up after your mess
Get out Uncle Sam
Haiti is our own

Haiti is our own

**Lyrics and music:
Jocelyn Hyppolite**

Haiti is our own

Haiti is our own

Written and harmonized by
Francis Saint-Hubert

Exiled from my sick Country

To life, liveliness, death
Nostalgia of the native land
Land of habits and costumes

Nostalgia of lives forms
Manners, good and bad
Exiled far from their country
And their unfulfilled loves

Exiled from my sick country

To life, liveliness, and lying ill
Cheerless, sluggish, languid
Overwhelm, distressed, frightened
Hopeless of tomorrow
Put aside in their country
Into the deep dark
Tormented prison hole

Exiled from my sick country

To death, dead blood, healed
Sleeping forever, liberated
Free of their anguished
Torments and regrets
Buried, relaxed at last
In those dark tombs
In the path of oblivion

Exiled from my sick country

I badly read your sheet music
Written in rebellion
Since you are departed
I trip from time to time
To that marching band music
In the path of the lost years
And of uncertain tomorrows

Exiled from my sick country

I would love to surpass
Your achievements
Rewrite your music in revolution
To build for us
That dreamed immensity
Exiled from my sick country
Since a long, long time

The Generals

I am strong
Extremely strong
Said the General
This is my time
The time of the Generals

AH! AH! AH! I am General

It's my turn to give orders
To pile up a lot of money
Pick up a few mistresses
On guard sergeant!
Gather my soldiers
I am going to make a mess,
Tremble little people!

AH! AH! AH! I am General

Crazy brains of sickness
Neurotic, mental atrophy
Sick narrow spirit
Confused and limited
Myopia, hallucinated

Visible ignorance
Noisy presence
Of course in fashion
Killer mentality
Cops mentality

Commander oppressors
Paranoiac aggressors
Trained murderers
Careers of expertise

General of the armed forces
General of the brigade
General of the dung
You are all murderers

Wind Blowing

Sure times have changed
In America Hitler has multiplied
At the Uncle Sam Congress
Gravediggers of democracy
Eloquent liars with quick answers
Everything is at nude to the sun

The UN is undressed
The OAS fingered
The International sold
Vatican denounced
The Soviets dismantled
The masses bluffed
Of their erroneous leadership

The Capital is bankrupt
Its structures are crumbling
On the weight of corruption
From thievery to murder
From plunder to waste

The new world order is in action
Surrounding a sand castle
It is disorder in permanence
The falling of dominoes
Down the scale
No more balance!
America is charging the world!

Yankee

You have dropped
Your children
On Hiroshima,
Nagasaki

Buried Patrice Lumumba
Ashed Allende
Robbed Puerto Rico
And named it
Commonwealth!

Made the Dominican Republic
Your baseball field
And your hen house
You have walked
Our land field
Without our permission

Stole our children's hope
And altered
Our meringue beats
Whenever your puppets
Are in control

You spread your greenery
While you are crying desperately
Against inflation

Hypocrite
In the name of the USA you came
Pretending to bring democracy
Peace and tranquility
Instead you brought
Trouble, misery, corruption, anarchy
And shame

You light up
The flame of destruction

Your own!

Unveil your face
Drop the curtain
International criminals

The Palestinians
Are not barbarians
If they are terrorists
They were
Well trained by you
Uncle Sam!

Professional invader!
Have you yet forgotten
The tears of Puerto Rico

69

Of Nicaragua in 1901?
The tears of homeless mothers
Hungry orphans
In Columbia in 1903?

The exploited
Worker's tears
Of the Dominican Republic
In 1905?

Have you forgotten
The blood thirsty land
The motherless
With empty stomachs
Of Cuba in 1906?

Have you yet forgotten
The groaning streets
Skinny dogs escaping before
The fears of your heavy boots…
In Nicaragua in 1911?

Have you yet forgotten
In Cuba the fallen comrades in 1912?

You have patrolled the entire planet
Established your empire.
Mexico in 1914
Haiti in 1915

70

Have you yet forgotten
The rebel attack
Of the Bay of Pigs
In 1961?

The massacre
Of the Dominican students
In 1965?
To kill at birth
The revolution embryo.

The pitiless invasion
Of Grenada in 1983?

Have you yet forgotten?
Bandit, conqueror,
Pirate, slave master
Or colonizer

You are a warmonger
Opposed everywhere
By everyone
Chased from Cuba
Vietnam, Cambodia
Laos, Iran
Nicaragua, Libya
Cornered everywhere
And by everyone
You are now expiate your crimes
FATHER OF TERRORISM!

71

The Vampire State

SPEEDING
Burning red light
Disorderly conduct
Reckless driving
Disobeying traffic signs
To name a few proscriptions.
Increasing our pain
Anger and blood pressure.
Siren, flashing lights!

PULL OVER!
STOP!
YOUR LICENSE
AND
REGISTRATIONS!!!

Guilty at birth
Guilty at sight
Guilty of color
Guilty of race
Guilty of language
Guilty of accent
GUILTY!

Sixty-seven pain,
Sixty-seven shame,

72

Sixty-seven humiliations,
Sixty-seven hard labor,
Sixty-seven tons of blood,

SILENCE!

Don't you dare
Make the judge angry
He could charge you
Up to five hundred
Five hundred democracy
Five hundred arbitrary
Five hundred times to steal
Legally
Properly

Honest workers
Five Hundred: times to suck
One's blood
And not worry a bit.
This is Dracula time
This is Dracula State
This is Vampire State
The Empire State
The divided State
But United States.
The state is separated
From the church
But the Bible is the work stone
In the courtroom

73

WHAT A TRAGEDY!

One must respect the law
The policeman swears an oath
To tell the truth
But the truth
So help him God…

He takes the stand
And lies his tail off
The judge nods his head
Satisfied with the lie
So well dressed
To resemble the truth
And said
I find the defendant *Guilty!*

Guilty, Guilty at birth
Guilty at sight and you know the song.
Society upside down
But everything is in order
In perfect order
It's standard harmony
In the symphonic orchestra

WHAT A SOCIETY!
All the human ressourses are asleep!

You know it is time to vomit.

(Drawing by Maxo Rimpel)

GUILTY!

It's Not Okay!

It's okay
Who can stop you?
From invading my country
And calling yourself
Freedom fighter

It's okay
You have been the world
Since Stalinism
Swallowed its pride
And sold out to you

It's okay
To fabricate the H-bomb
The N-bomb, missiles
Aircrafts, all weaponry
To maintain your domination

It's okay
To buy me
With your dollar
Bill of shame,
Crime and prostitution

It's okay
"In God We Trust"
Your green is printed
Amen to that
Trust the mighty green God

It's okay
To drug me
Your created God
Is my opium key
To escape your infernal world?

It's okay
To promise me
Heaven after death
While you enjoy
Your good happy
Long life on earth

It's not okay
To rise up against
Your precious interest
Which is more vital
Than the rest of the world

It's not okay
To defend ourselves
Against your aggression
It's an offense
Even worse an insult
To fight back

It's not okay
To develop our country
To the extent of
Becoming self-sufficient
To a potential competitor

It's not okay
To want my piece
Of the pie now!
To demand my share now
While I am still alive.
While I am still alive
Damn it, it's not okay!
Your *INJUSTICE*

LIVE AGAIN

I f I should live again
I 'll be looking for you
Wherever you may be
on our planet
Living again
I'll sing for you my dear
My pain and misery

I would say to you
How much I love you!
How I adore you!
I would love to love you dear!
I would say to you
How deep I love you
How I adore you still

You may have a new face
Maybe a new name too
I'll still recognize you
From a Gladys or a Solange
Oh! Yes indeed I would
The day we would meet again

You could say I'm insane
I am off reality
What about love and life,
And suffering
How real are they?
Let alone a fatality
Like death itself

Let me tell you still
How much I love you!
How I adore you!
I would love to love you dear!
Let me tell you still
How deep I love you!
How I adore you still.

Live again

Lyrics and music:
Jocelyn Hyppolite

If I should live a - gain

I'll be look - ing for you

where - e - ver you may be _____ on our pla-

net _____ li - ving a - gain.

2

Live again

Live again

how deep I love you   how I a-dore you

still. ————   You may have a   new

Written and harmonized by:
Francis Saint-Hubert

Hands off

Youve have eaten my sugar
You have drunk my coffee
My blood too for that matter
So many, many times before

You have slept in my bed
Eaten in my dishes
And kicked me in the teeth
So many, many times before

You have used my sisters
Corrupted my brothers
Made a fool of everyone of us
So many, many times before

You have dug in my soil
Taken my bauxite
My gold and copper
But to take Haïti, Yankees
You must leave your skin

In the name of the United Nations
You brought modern occupation
To protect your friendly bourgeoisie
Against the Haïtian masses
Hands off Yankees!

Haïti is not for sale
Haïti is my sovereign country
Haïti is all my pride, Yankees
Haïti is all my soul and dignity
Hands off Yankees!

Reality

When one comes
To analyze deeply
Life, society
And its surrounding
You feel the burden
That heavy load of pain
You're eager to fight
For a change
To move and remove
The sweat of stress and pain
When caught by
The old age of time
One must say "time out"
And take a deep breath
Of fresh air
Because too much awareness
Can be so scary.

The Eagle

Twenty-five
twenty-six
twenty-seven
Dad?
eight, nine
Dad?
Don't interrupt!
Thirty, thirty-one
two, three
four.
How come?
That is what
I tried to tell
you dad!
No, no, no
What happenned
to my chicken?
The big, big bird
took two
of them dad!

You mean
that damn eagle?
Yeah dad!
I'm going to kill
that eagle
Give me
my shot gun
let me
blast his A...
But dad,
the government
will get on your case.
The government
does not buy
me my chicken!
The eagle is an
endangered
species dad!

Endangered
species my F!
Endangered
species my A!
Shoot the eagle!
He is a vulture.
Shoot the eagle!
The eagle
is a killer.
Shoot the eagle!
The eagle is a bird
of prey
Shoot the eagle!

The eagle is the
farmer's pain.
Shoot the eagle!
Shoot the eagle!
Shoot, shoot, shoot!
Shoot the eagle!

My obsession

Since I met you
My heartbeat
Seems to change
Its rhythmic pattern

Hearing your voice
Seeing your silhouette
Seeing your face
Seeing you move
Seeing you walk
Has a tremendous
Impact on my emotions
That cuts
My breathing habit
In so many small
Pieces of breath
Makes me wonder
Why Cupid gave you
So much power over me

And then on day
You went away

Since, my Dear
My imagination
Tricks me, torments me
Your image is fixed
In my memory
I have become
Demented, hallucinating
Any street corner
Any space of time
At any moment
I'll see a Hispanic woman

To her, I'll lend
Your face
Your facial emotion
Your facial expression
Your fury
Your smile
Your laughter
Your grace
Your charm
Your sensuality

Your body shape
Your movement
Your walk
Your fashion
Your complexion

My dear friend
Your absence
Hurts me!
Shakes me!
Troubles me so deeply
That I can
Close my eyes
And see you
Coming to me
As if I'm dreaming
In broad daylight
Every day of the week
Every week of the month
Every month of the year.

Alphabetical index of poems

Printed in the United States
by Baker & Taylor Publisher Services